# DO BEARS SLEEP ALL WINTER?

## Questions and Answers About Bears

BY MELVIN AND GILDA BERGER

ILLUSTRATED BY ROBERTO OSTI

SCHOLASTIC NONFICTION

# CONTENTS

Introduction • 3

THE BEAR FACTS • 4

THE WORLD OF BEARS • 22

BEARS AND HUMANS • 40

Index • 48

About the Authors and Illustrator • 48

**KEY TO ABBREVIATIONS**

cm = centimeter/centimetre
kg = kilogram
km = kilometer/kilometre
kph = kilometers/kilometres per hour
m = meter/metre
t = tonne

Text copyright © 2001 by Melvin and Gilda Berger
Illustrations copyright © 2001 by Roberto Osti
All rights reserved. Published by Scholastic Inc.
SCHOLASTIC, SCHOLASTIC NONFICTION, and associated logos are trademarks and/or
registered trademarks of Scholastic Inc.

*Library of Congress Cataloging-in-Publication Data available*

ISBN-13: 978-0-439-26671-0
ISBN-10: 0-439-26671-8

*Book design by David Saylor and Nancy Sabato*

12 11 10 9 8 7 6 5 4 3          9 10 11 12/0

Printed in the U.S.A.                   08
First printing, January 2002
This edition first printing, October 2007

Expert reader: Don Moore, Ph.D.
Curator of Animals
Wildlife Conservation Society
Central Park Wildlife Center
New York, NY

*The bears on the cover are grizzly bears. The bears on the title page are giant pandas.
The bear cub on page 3 is an American black bear.*

For Matty, who saw bears in the wilds of Alaska
— M. AND G. BERGER

For Julia
— R. OSTI

# INTRODUCTION

**B**ears have always been very important to us. For thousands of years, people have worshiped the bear. Some still do.

The word *bear* occurs in many of our everyday expressions. For example, when you are very hungry, you might say you're "as hungry as a bear." When you carry something you "bear" it. When you are brave, you "bear up." When you "bear down" on something you press on it.

The Chicago Bears are a football team. The Boston Bruins (*bruin* is another word for bear) play hockey. The Chicago Cubs are a baseball team.

Bears are the state animal of Arkansas, California, Kentucky, Montana, New Mexico, Texas, and West Virginia. The bear is also the provincial animal of New Brunswick, Nova Scotia, and Quebec in Canada. California and Missouri show bears on their state flags.

Why do bears mean so much to us? Perhaps it's because they remind us of ourselves:

- Bears are smart, curious, and playful.
- Most bears like sweets and eat the same foods we do.
- Bears sit up and eat with their hands (paws).
- Many bears can walk on two legs.
- Almost all bears snore.

*Do Bears Sleep All Winter?* brings you many amazing facts about bears. So "bear with us" as we tell you everything you want to know about bears!

*Melvin Berger   Gilda Berger*

# THE BEAR FACTS

## Do bears sleep all winter?

Some do. These bears settle down for a long, long sleep. It lasts all through the cold winter months.

When asleep, a bear's heartbeat and breathing slow down. Its body grows somewhat cooler. And the bear doesn't eat, drink, or get rid of body wastes the entire time!

## Do the sleeping bears sometimes wake up?

Yes. Noises or disturbances may awaken them. On warm days they sometimes get up and take a stroll. Then they go back to sleep.

Many people say bears hibernate (HIE-buhr-nayt). But most scientists disagree. They say a bear's winter sleep is not the same as true hibernation.

## What is true hibernation?

A much deeper winter sleep. True hibernators, such as bats, frogs, snakes, turtles, and woodchucks, sleep far more soundly than bears do. They don't wake by themselves. It's almost impossible to awaken them. And their heartbeats, breathing, and body temperatures go way down.

## Do bears snore?

Almost all do.

Asiatic black bear

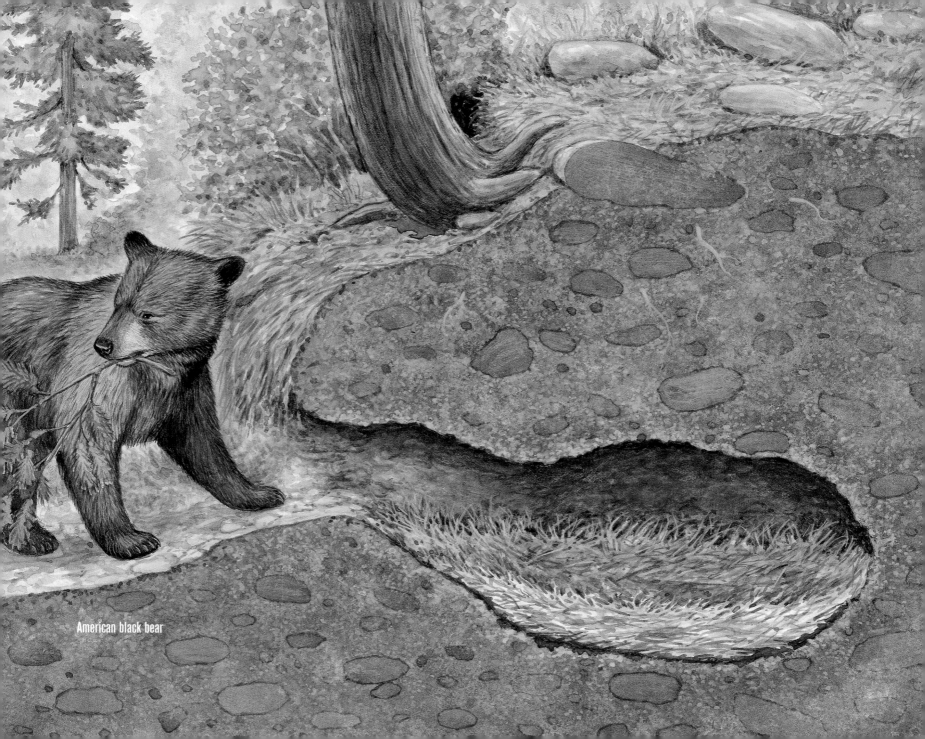

American black bear

## When do bears get ready for their winter sleep?

In the early fall. The bears stuff themselves with fish, mice, deer, berries, and other food. Each day they take in an amazing 20,000 calories. That's just like you gulping down 100 hamburgers in a single day!

Some female bears more than double their weight. Male and female bears add as much as 8 inches (20.3 cm) of fat to their bodies. This thick layer of extra fat under the skin will help the bears keep warm during the cold winter months. The fat will also provide them with the nutrition they need during their winter sleep.

## Where do the bears sleep all winter?

Mostly in dens. Some bears dig dens under big boulders or tree roots. A bear may have to move 1 ton (1 t) of soil to get the job done!

Other bears tunnel their dens into hillsides or build shelters of twigs and branches. Pregnant polar bears scoop out ice and snow to make their dens.

## What do dens look like?

They differ. But most dens have an entrance, a short, narrow tunnel, and an open living space or chamber just large enough for the bear. Of course, the bigger the bear, the bigger the den. The "mattress" is usually a soft layer of grass, leaves, pine needles, and tree branches—up to 9 inches (22.8 cm) thick.

## Do bears sleep in the same den each winter?

Some do. Others prepare a new den every year. Some even take over dens dug by other bears.

Bears crawl into their dens when the weather turns cold and food is hard to find. Once inside, the bear curls up and starts its long winter snooze.

## How long do bears sleep?

As long as six months. In their winter dens, half-asleep pregnant bears give birth to their babies.

Bear babies are called cubs. Their mothers and all female bears are called she-bears or sows; their fathers and all male bears are known as boars.

## When are the cubs born?

Usually in January or February. The average size of a litter is two cubs. But as many as five may be born at the same time.

At first, the mother holds the cubs snugly against her body to warm them. She feeds them her rich milk, then licks and cleans them.

## How big are the cubs at birth?

Tiny. Most bear cubs are only about 8 inches (20.3 cm) long and weigh less than 1 pound (0.4 kg)—the size of a small squirrel.

Newborn cubs are helpless. They cannot see, hear, smell, or walk, and they have no teeth. At birth, all cubs—except polar bear cubs—have little or no fur to keep them warm.

## How fast do cubs grow?

Very fast! After a few weeks, the cubs open their eyes and soon take their first steps. Baby bears have blue eyes.

The cubs nurse, or drink the mother bear's milk. They may gain as many as several pounds (kilograms) a day!

The little cubs have lots of growing to do. Most adult bears are about 5 feet (1.5 m) long and weigh 300 pounds (140 kg). But big brown bears reach lengths of 9 feet (2.7 m) and weigh a staggering 1,700 pounds (770 kg)!

American black bear and cubs

## Do the cubs also leave the dens?

Yes. The she-bears push their cubs out of the dens ahead of them. The furry little cubs quickly learn to play. Soon they're running, jumping, climbing, wrestling, and rolling on the ground—just like human children!

## Are mother bears good parents?

Yes. But a mother bear is very strict. If the cubs don't follow her signals to "Stay there" or "Come down," the she-bear swats them with her paw!

The mother bear continues to feed the cubs milk from her body for between two months and three years. As the cubs grow bigger, she also leads them toward various foods to taste—plants and berries, fruits and honey, and fish and small animals.

From the mother bear, the cubs learn ways to get food and keep safe. By copying what she does, they discover how to catch salmon, pick fruit, find insects, and much, much more. They find out when to flee or scoot up a tree.

Grizzly bear and cubs

## Do mother bears teach the cubs to climb?

No. All bears (except polar bears) climb naturally. They do not need to learn.

To climb a tree, bears grasp the tree trunk with their front legs and pull themselves up—much as inchworms do. But bears are much faster. Larger bears sometimes "ladder" up by using the tree branches as rungs. They walk down backward, sliding or jumping down from low limbs.

## How long do cubs stay with their mothers?

It varies. American black and polar bear cubs stay close to their mothers for at least one winter after their birth. Brown bear cubs usually stick close to home for three winters before going off on their own. Most cubs take 5 to 10 years to reach their full size.

The second or third summer is the most dangerous time in a bear cub's life. Not yet fully grown, the young bears are likely prey for bigger bears, dogs, wolves, and humans.

American black bear

## Where do bears sleep the rest of the year?

In day beds. Black bears make their day beds in two ways. Either they bend tree branches high up in a tree, or build them out of broken limbs on the ground. Brown bears nap in a grassy place or on a nest of pine needles. And in winter, polar bears scoop out pits in the snow for their day beds. Brrr! They really need their thick fur for sleeping on snow.

## Do bears like sweets?

Yes. Bears like honey and almost every other plant and animal food. The bears' 42 teeth look like our teeth. The front ones are sharp for tearing apart meat or hard plant materials. The back ones are flat for grinding up the food in the bears' mouths. A sugary diet makes bears among the few wild animals with tooth cavities!

## How do bears find food?

Mostly by smell. It is a bear's most important sense. Bears use their large nostrils to sniff out odors. Some say a bear's ability to detect scents is 100 times better than that of a human!

One American black bear in California, for example, followed an odor for 3 miles (4.8 km)—straight to the body of a dead deer. Polar bears have an even keener sense of smell. They can pick up the scent of a seal from 20 miles (32 km) away!

## Do bears have sharp eyesight?

No. Bears are probably nearsighted. Experts think that's why bears go up close to strange objects. They want to see them better. Some people think that bears can recognize moving objects more easily than objects that are still. Bears also stand up on two legs to see farther.

Scientists believe bears have fairly good hearing. In tests, they found that bears pick up the sounds of normal human conversation from about 1,000 feet (300 m) away. Bears turn and look if someone cocks a gun or takes a photo at 164 feet (50 m).

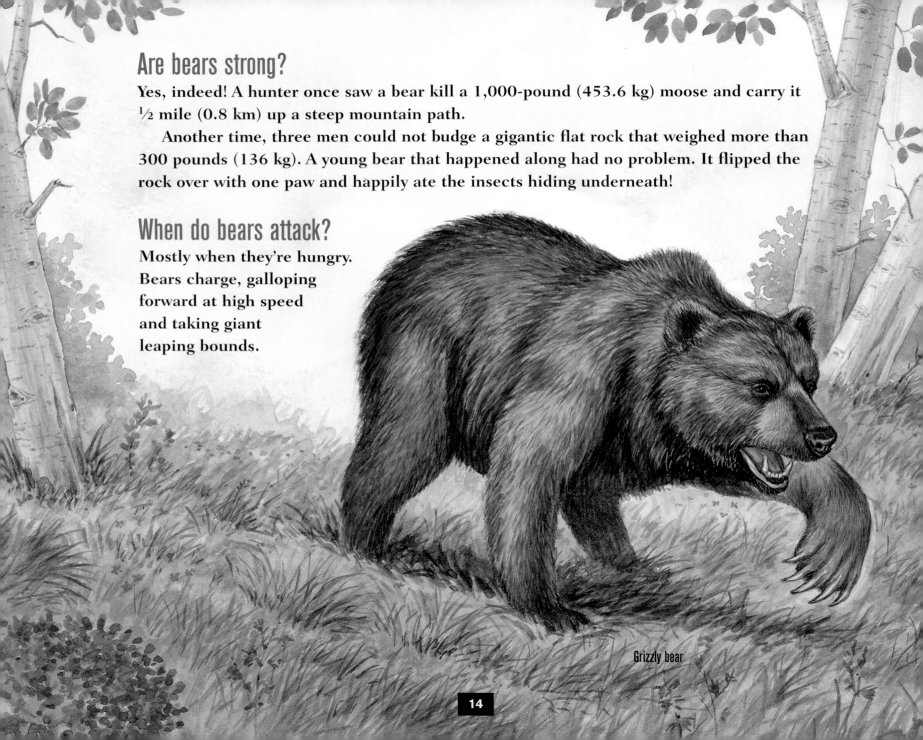

## Are bears strong?

Yes, indeed! A hunter once saw a bear kill a 1,000-pound (453.6 kg) moose and carry it ½ mile (0.8 km) up a steep mountain path.

Another time, three men could not budge a gigantic flat rock that weighed more than 300 pounds (136 kg). A young bear that happened along had no problem. It flipped the rock over with one paw and happily ate the insects hiding underneath!

## When do bears attack?

Mostly when they're hungry. Bears charge, galloping forward at high speed and taking giant leaping bounds.

Grizzly bear

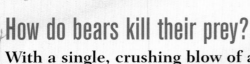

## How do bears kill their prey?

With a single, crushing blow of a front paw. One whack is often enough to kill a large moose, elk, or deer. But sometimes the prey survives. Then the bear lunges forward and sinks its teeth into the victim's neck.

The bear's strong, curved claws—from about 2½ to 6 inches (6.3 to 15.2 cm) long—are another deadly weapon. These sharp hooks can rip through the skin of any animal.

A bear's claws are always out, ready to strike and slice its prey or foes. Bears can't pull their claws back like cats, lions, or tigers can.

## Do bears give "bear hugs"?

No. Bears rarely rear up on two legs and grasp their victims or enemies in "bear hugs." Yet it sometimes looks that way.

Bears sometimes do stand when attacking their victims. But they do not grasp them. In this position, the bears can more easily wallop their prey with a front paw. Standing is also better for biting.

Young elk

## Can bears run fast?

Yes. A bear's large size and loose skin make it look slow and clumsy. But don't judge a bear by its looks! Bears can put on amazing bursts of speed. When chasing prey, some bears can reach speeds as fast as 35 miles an hour (56 kph). That's about as fast as a car driving on a city street. It's much faster than a human runner. And a running bear can race at high speed for 10 miles (16 km) without a rest!

## Can bears walk on two paws?

Yes, but only for short distances. Bears mostly walk on four paws. But they sometimes stand on two feet to sniff the air, look around, grab food, or attack an enemy.

Most four-legged animals walk and run on their toes. But bears put the entire soles of their feet flat on the ground—like humans do. Each sole has a thick pad that grows back as it wears down.

## Can bears run downhill without falling?

Yes. People once thought that bears could not run down a hill without tripping. But that's not true. Bears can travel down a steep hill without any trouble.

## Do bears like water?

Yes. All bears seem to like water and are great swimmers. They hurry along using the "dog paddle." And when they're done, they dry off with doglike shakes.

Bears plunge into the water to catch fish or other water creatures. They seek out streams, lakes, ponds, rivers, or the ocean to escape insects, cool off, relieve an itch, or maybe just to have some fun. When they're not swimming, bears often just sit and splash.

European brown bear

Asiatic brown bear

## How many kinds of fur do bears have?

Two. Close to their skin, bears have soft, short hairs, called underfur. This layer helps keep the bears warm in the winter and cool in the summer. Sticking up above the underfur are stiff, long, guard hairs. They protect the bears from insects and dirt. A thin coating of oil on both the underfur and guard hairs keeps water from reaching the bears' skin.

Most bears' fur also acts as camouflage. Black or brown fur helps bears blend in with their forest surroundings. The white fur of polar bears makes them hard to see against snow and ice. Only the giant pandas' bright white-and-black fur makes them very easy to spot.

## Do bears shed their fur?

Yes. Every spring or summer, bears molt, or shed their fur. To help rid themselves of the old coat, the bears rub against trees and rocks. This also helps to mark the bears' territory, letting other bears know that they are there.

Bears look quite messy while they are molting. Large chunks of hair hang down, and the bears look ragged and tattered. But while the old coat is being shed, a new fur coat is growing. By fall, the bears look terrific.

## How long do bears live?

About 24 years in the wild. Bears in zoos live longer because they have plenty of food, protection from enemies, and good medical care. Many reach about 40 years of age.

Scientists can tell a bear's age at the time of its death. They remove and look at a section of one tooth under a microscope. The tooth has a number of tiny rings, one for each year of a bear's life. Counting the number of rings in a bear's tooth tells its age. It's like counting the rings in a tree trunk to find the age of the tree.

## Do bears live alone or in groups?

Mostly alone. Bears come together only during mating time. Unlike the bear family in the story "Goldilocks and the Three Bears," the mother bears raise their cubs by themselves.

## How do bears keep in touch?

With sound. Cubs whimper when upset, cry when hurt, hum when nursing, and hiss when scared. Mother bears and cubs call to one another when separated. Adult bears roar to warn away an enemy or when disturbed or angry.

Generally speaking, forest bears call more often and make more sounds than bears that live in open country. The reason is that trees prevent them from seeing one another. Now you can guess why polar bears are among the quietest bears of all.

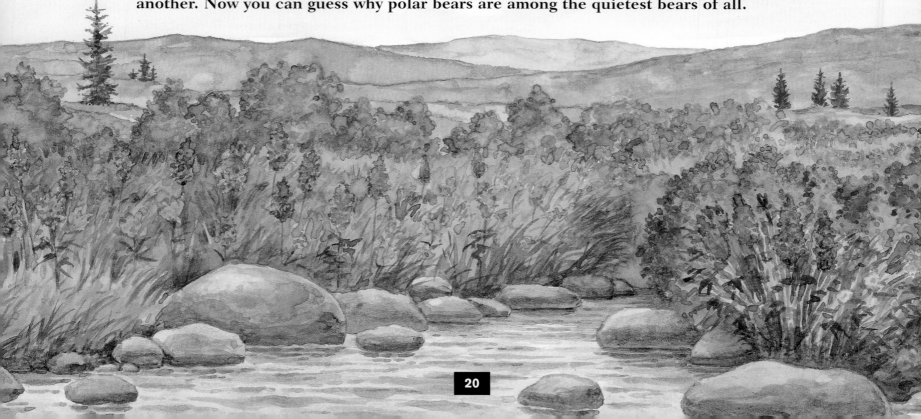

# Are bears noisy?

No. Bears are usually silent and use body language to communicate. A bear may bend its neck, stare, or blow wet bubbles at another bear to signal anger. Lying down, lowering the head, or backing up are ways to show fear or respect for another bear.

Many bears rub against trees or rocks to mark their territory and warn others away. American black bears and grizzly bears sometimes stand up on their hind legs and make deep scratch marks in the bark of trees with their front claws. This shows the boundaries of their space.

Grizzly bear and cubs

# THE WORLD OF BEARS

## When did the first bears appear on Earth?

About 27 million years ago. Fossils show that the first bears probably showed up in present-day Europe. They looked like a mixture of dog and bear. And they were about the size of today's fox terrier dogs.

As time passed, the bears changed. They grew bigger and stronger. The tails of the early bears disappeared. Over millions of years, bears developed into different species, or kinds, of bear. Their bodies and ways of living are suited for the various places they lived.

## What are cave bears?

A species of bear that lived from about 60,000 to 10,000 years ago—and then disappeared. Cave bears made their homes in natural caves or tunnels in the ground.

Like some bears today, cave bears slept all winter in these simple shelters. They also gave birth to their cubs there.

Sometimes human cave dwellers lived in the same large caves as the bears. The caves were warm and dry. The sleeping bears were easy targets for the early hunters.

## Why did the cave bears disappear?

No one knows for sure. Overhunting of the bears for food and fur may be one reason. Hunters killed tremendous numbers of cave bears, mostly during the bears' winter sleep.

Also, the cave bears died out around the end of the Ice Age about 10,000 years ago. Some think the cave bears were not able to adapt to the warmer climate.

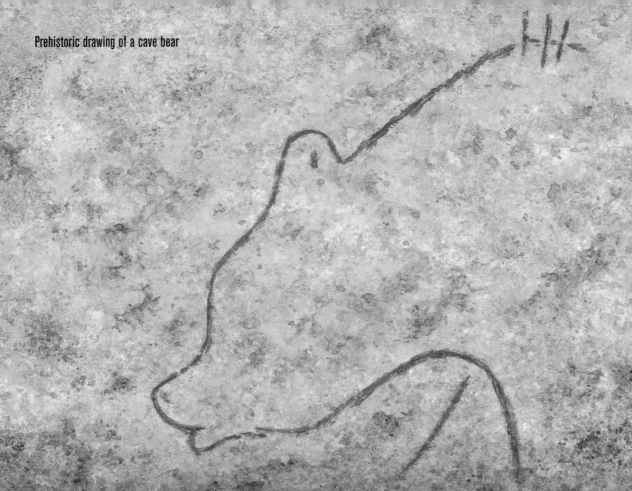

Prehistoric drawing of a cave bear

## Where do bears live today?

All around the world—except Africa, Australia, and Antarctica.

Bears belong to eight main species. The four large kinds of bears are: brown bears in North America, Europe, and Asia; polar bears in the polar regions around the North Pole and the Arctic Ocean; American black bears in North America; and giant panda bears in China.

The four somewhat smaller species are: Asiatic black bears in Asia; sloth bears in India; spectacled bears in South America; and sun bears in southern Asia.

Grizzly bear fishing for salmon

## Which are the biggest bears?

Brown bears. The heaviest male on record weighed more than 1 ton (1 t)—2,500 pounds (1,134 kg). He was 10 feet (3 m) long—about as long as an automobile. As with all kinds of bears, the females weigh less and are smaller than the males.

Brown bears are the most widespread bear species. They are not in danger of disappearing even though their numbers have dropped by half since the mid-1800s.

## Which brown bears are the best known?

Grizzly bears. These bears live on the mountains and in the big open spaces of the western United States and Canada. Their name comes from the silvery white hairs that grow in their long, thick brown fur. The word *grizzled* means "streaked with gray."

A typical grizzly weighs from 300 to 860 pounds (135 to 390 kg). You can tell a grizzly by the large hump of fat and muscles on its shoulders. This gives it powerful front paws for striking other animals with killing force.

## What do grizzlies eat?

It varies. In spring, the grizzly bears feed on baby animals, such as deer, elk, and caribou. But in summer, they mostly nibble grass and other plants and dig for roots with their long, sharp claws. Come fall, the grizzlies' diet shifts to berries and often salmon. The fish supply the bears with enough fat to carry them through their long winter sleep.

## What are Kodiak bears?

Another type of brown bear that lives in North America. Thousands of years ago, you could only find Kodiak bears on Kodiak Island off the coast of Alaska. Today, Kodiak bears live on the Alaskan mainland as well.

## Which bears are called sea bears?

Polar bears. They live along the coasts, on islands, and on floating pieces of ice in the Arctic Ocean.

Polar bears have the most fur of any species of bear. Except for the nose and paw pads, they are completely covered with a coat of thick yellowish-white fur. Each hair is a hollow, see-through tube that lets sunlight through to warm the bear's black skin. Air trapped inside the hairs also helps to hold in the bear's body heat and keep out the icy cold.

## Are polar bears good swimmers?

The best! Polar bears swim great distances in their search for food. Sailors have seen them swim hour after hour at a steady 6 miles an hour (9.6 kph) without stopping. They can dive and stay underwater for up to two minutes!

Strips of skin connect parts of the toes of a polar bear's front paws. The webbing helps the paws work like paddles and adds to the bears' swimming speed.

## Do polar bears travel across ice?

Yes. A polar bear walks or runs much farther than most other kinds of bears. One polar bear may cover as many as 43 miles (70 km) in a single day! That's like walking from Washington, D.C., to Baltimore, Maryland, in one day.

Short, stiff hairs on the soles of the polar bears' paws let them walk and run on ice without slipping. The nonskid paw fur also helps to keep their feet warm.

## What is a polar bear's favorite food?

Seal. The bear often waits by a seal's breathing hole in the ice. Sooner or later the seal comes up for air. The bear grabs it with its powerful paws. One yank, and the bear pulls the seal up through the hole and onto the ice.

Polar bears

American black bear

## Which bear is most common in North America?

The American black bear. Today, more than 700,000 black bears live in Canada and the United States. Of these, about 75,000 roam U.S. national parks and forests.

Because of the large number of American black bears, some states allow hunting during certain seasons. Hunters kill perhaps 25,000 black bears every year.

## What color are American black bears?

Black or brown or other colors. Many American black bears have rusty brown fur and are called cinnamon bears. One kind, the glacier bear of Alaska, has gray hairs mixed with the black, making its coat look bluish. And the ghost or Kermode's bear of Canada has creamy white fur and white claws.

Male American black bears weigh from 130 to 660 pounds (60 to 300 kg). Even so, they are the smallest bears in North America.

## Are American black bears smart?

Yes. Black bears are fast learners and quickly get used to change. They can use their short, sharp claws very skillfully. Campers like to tell stories of the bears' talent for opening screw-top jars and locked coolers!

## Are American black bears good tree climbers?

Yes. From the time they are young cubs, the bears climb to play, to search for food such as beehives or bird's nests, or to sleep.

Climbing is also the main way American black bear cubs escape their enemies. The cubs go far out on thin branches. Larger enemies don't follow the cubs because they know the branch will break and they'll tumble to the ground.

## Where do giant pandas live?

In the bamboo forests of China. The giant pandas are shy, stocky bears with large heads.

Each day, pandas swallow as much as 44 pounds (20 kg) of bamboo—their chief food. The pandas' paws are well adapted to eating bamboo. Each front paw has a special bone, a kind of thumb, which is perfect for grasping thin bamboo stems. The pandas' huge molars are excellent for grinding bamboo shoots. Small wonder that *panda* is a word used in the Himalayas that means "bamboo eater."

In recent years, people have cleared the bamboo forests in China and built homes and farms on the land. Without a place to live, giant pandas have become very rare. Today, there are fewer than 1,000 giant pandas left in the wild!

## Are giant pandas true bears?

Yes. Giant pandas look like bears and walk flat-footed just as other bears do. They mate and give birth to cubs in a bearlike way. And if you took a look inside the mouth of a giant panda, you would find 42 teeth—the same number as most bears have.

## Why are they called "giant" pandas?

To separate them from the much smaller red, or lesser, pandas. Red pandas are reddish-brown animals with bushy, ringed tails. They live in the same places as giant pandas and eat the same food. But lesser pandas are not bears like giant pandas. Lesser pandas may be relatives of raccoons.

Giant panda

Asiatic black bear

## Which bears are sometimes called moon bears?

Asiatic black bears. Their nickname comes from the white crescent mark that looks like a new moon on their shaggy black chests.

Thick, hairy manes around their necks and shoulders give these bears of eastern Asia a special look. And they have big, round ears that stick out above their heads. Although they're about the same length as American black bears, Asiatic black bears are usually thinner and aren't as heavy.

## Where do Asiatic black bears spend most of their time?

Usually up in high forest trees. Asiatic black bears rest on day beds they form from tree branches. They can also be found in caves and crevices. This keeps them safe from enemies—both human and animal.

## Are Asiatic black bears friendly?

Not at all. Asiatic black bears can be fierce. When threatened, these ferocious bears will attack cattle and horses—and sometimes people.

Sloth bear

## Where did the sloth bear get its name?

From its slow, sluggish way of moving. Sloth bears take their name from *sloth*, an Old English word that means "slow."

## Can sloth bears move quickly?

Sometimes. Sloth bears get sudden bursts of energy—especially if disturbed. When frightened, the sloth bear suddenly springs into action. Then it gallops with leaps, and moves faster than a running human.

## Where do sloth bears live?

In warm climates. Their long, shaggy, and usually matted fur always looks like it could use a good brushing. Their fur is jet black with a white or light brown horseshoe-shaped patch on the chest. Their bellies and underlegs have little or no fur.

Sloth bears mostly hunt for food at night. Among the foods they seek are insects, eggs, fruit, flowers, and dead animals. A favorite is honey, which is why sloth bears are sometimes called honey bears. Their long fur protects them from stings when they try to steal the bees' honey.

## Which insects do sloth bears mostly feed on?

Termites. To get the termites, the sloth bear rips open a termite nest—usually in a rotten log—with its long, hooklike claws. It then forms its flat tongue and lips into a long tube and blows away the wood chips. Plunging its snout into the smashed nest, the sloth bear sucks up the fleeing termites. But the bear has terrible manners. You can hear its loud snorting and slurping noises as far away as 300 feet (100 m)!

# Which is the only species of bear in South America?

The spectacled bear. These bears are generally found in the cool, humid forests of the Andes Mountains. But spectacled bears also live in grasslands and dry regions.

   Spectacled bears have a circle or half circle of white fur around their eyes that look like spectacles, or eyeglasses. The markings are so unique that scientists can use them to tell one spectacled bear from another.

Spectacled bear

## What do spectacled bears eat?

Fruit, tree leaves, and the leaves of bromeliads (broh-MILL-ee-adz), plants that grow on trees. Spectacled bears are excellent climbers. They easily make their way up tree trunks to reach their food. Often, the branches bend as they search for something to eat. The bears then use the bent branches to form a day bed in the tree.

Spectacled bears eat more plant food than most species of bears. In summer, when fruit is ripening, this kind of bear may remain in a tree for several days, happily chewing the fruit.

## What do spectacled bears feed on in the desert?

Different kinds of cactus plants. But you can be sure that they don't make day beds out of sharp, prickly cacti!

Sun bear

## Which are the world's smallest bears?

Sun bears. Most sun bears have a top weight of 100 pounds (45 kg). The head is short and flat, with small beady eyes, a soft snout, and a very long, thin tongue. They measure only about 3 to 4 feet (1 to 1.4 m) long. Their black fur is unusually thick for animals that live in the tropics. And the soles of their paws have no hair at all.

Ancient people named these bears for their yellow chest marking that looks like the rising sun. Since these bears resemble dogs, they are sometimes called dog bears. And some people call them Malay bears, after the language spoken in Southeast Asia where the bears live.

## How do sun bears spend their days?

Sleeping and sunbathing in tree day beds. The bears build the beds high above the ground. They break or bend tree branches into platforms that can hold their weight. Then sun bears lie down on their bellies to rest.

The sun bears' powerful front legs, very large paws, and long, curved claws suit them very well for climbing trees. They can nearly hang upside down by their claws, which are more curved and sharp than any other bears'. Their small size and light weight also help.

## What do sun bears do at night?

Hunt for food. Sun bears eat a wide variety of foods that grow in the jungle. Fruit, palm leaf tips, termites, and small animals and birds make up their diet.

## Are sun bears dangerous?

They can be. Older sun bears are said to be bad-tempered and dangerous. Yet they normally attack only to defend themselves. When fighting, they bark loudly.

# BEARS AND HUMANS

## What is the Cult of the Bear?

A religion of cave-dwelling people. Followers belonged to many groups and cultures. They worshiped the bear from about 60,000 to 11,000 years ago. The Cult of the Bear was one of the earliest faiths in the world.

Every fall, the people saw the bears "die," or go into their winter sleep. Then, in the spring, they saw the bears "come back to life," or wake from their sleep. They thought, "Bears are magical creatures. They die and are then reborn." This belief began the Cult of the Bear. Believers held that if you ate the flesh of a bear, you would be immortal, or live forever.

## Do people still honor bears?

Yes. The Hopi Indians of the southwestern United States consider the bear kachina, or spirit, to be sacred. In special ceremonies, men wear bear kachina masks and perform dances to cure the sick, bring rain, or make corn grow.

Other native North American peoples honor the bear in different ways: Pueblo Indians use eagle feathers to paint a bear on the doors of rooms used for solemn rituals; Coos Indians do a bear dance to celebrate a girl's becoming a woman; Yokuts Indians' bear dancing is a way to give thanks for a good crop; Ute Indians welcome the coming of spring with three days of bear dancing and feasting.

The Inuit of northern Canada worship the polar bear. At certain times of the year they kill one and hang its bladder indoors. People bring offerings of food and drink to the bladder. According to Inuit belief, the bear's soul, or *innua*, is in its bladder.

## Do other countries celebrate bears?

Yes, many do. In Austria, Hungary, and Poland people celebrate Bear's Day on the same day we celebrate Groundhog Day. According to tradition, sleeping bears come out of their dens on February 2. If the bear sees its shadow, they say, there will be six more weeks of winter.

On Sakhalin Island and the Kuril Islands off the coast of Japan, each December, the Ainu people have a ritual festival in which they kill an Asiatic black bear cub. They believe that this returns the slain bear's soul to the spirit world from which it came. The Ainu follow the sacred ceremony with dancing and feasting.

Figure of a bear carved on a totem pole

## Which are the "bear constellations"?

Ursa Major, or the Great Bear, and Ursa Minor, or the Little Bear. The two constellations move in a counterclockwise direction around the North Star. Since the beginning of history, sailors, explorers, and world travelers have used the North Star and these constellations to find their direction.

The Big Dipper is part of Ursa Major. The Little Dipper is made up of most of the stars of Ursa Minor. To find the North Star, look for the bright star at the end of the handle of the Little Dipper.

## Where did Ursa Major and Ursa Minor get their names?

From Greek mythology. According to legend, Zeus fell in love with Callisto, a beautiful young goddess. His wife, Hera, grew jealous and turned Callisto into a bear. Callisto's son, Arcas, not knowing what had happened, raised his spear to kill the "bear." Zeus saved Callisto by changing Arcas into a bear, too. Then he placed them both in the sky—Callisto as Ursa Major, Arcas as Ursa Minor.

## Which star seems to follow the bear constellations?

The star Arcturus (ark-TEW-russ). This star is well known for its bright orange color. It is the fourth brightest star in the sky.

The Greeks named the star Arcturus, meaning "bear keeper," because it seems to follow Ursa Major and Ursa Minor across the sky. Arcturus is in the constellation Boötes (boh-OH-teez), called the Herdsman or the Bear Driver. In one legend, the gods ordered Boötes to follow Callisto and her son, the Little Bear, to keep them in their orbits. This explains the staff, or bear-prod, he holds in his hand.

American black bear

## Who first used bears for entertainment?

The ancient Romans. They forced bears into bloody battles with attack dogs or trained gladiators. The gladiators were usually armed with swords, spears, or bows and arrows. The fights often went on until the death of either the bear, the dogs, or the gladiators.

Starting in the Middle Ages, people paid to see bears perform like humans. In these entertainments, trained bears danced, rode horses or bicycles, played musical instruments, drank from bottles, swung on swings, or walked on tightropes.

## Do bears still perform today?

Yes. In India, Turkey, Greece, and elsewhere, trained bears perform as dancing bears. Most of the so-called "shows" take place on the street. Passersby throw coins into the bear trainers' cups. Many people think that forcing bears to dance is cruel and unkind.

In the United States, circus trainers often work with Asiatic black bears. These bears can be very playful and show excellent balance and coordination. But even trained bears are not tame and remain dangerous and unpredictable.

## Do bears often attack humans?

No. Bear attacks on people are surprisingly rare. The animals are very shy by nature. Most try to avoid humans, if possible.

A recent study of 230 encounters between brown bears and humans found that: the bears walked away 200 times; 23 times the bears paid no attention to the people; 5 times the bears threatened the humans but did not strike. Only twice did the bears actually attack.

However, as encounters increase, experts expect that the number of injuries to humans will increase.

## Where did the teddy bear get its name?

From President Theodore (Teddy, for short) Roosevelt. The president was a hunter who once refused to shoot a small bear cub. A toymaker, Morris Michton, made a toy version of the little bear and called it Teddy. Now, more than 100 years later, the teddy bear is still a beloved toy.

## What is Smokey Bear?

The symbol of fire prevention in the United States. The first Smokey Bear appeared in a 1944 poster for the United States Forest Service. It showed a cute little bear cub pouring water on a campfire.

About six years later, a fire broke out in New Mexico's Lincoln National Forest. Firefighters rescued a terrified little American black bear cub from the blaze. They named the bear Smokey and placed it in the National Zoo in Washington, D.C. This Smokey Bear lived until 1976.

## Who is Winnie-the-Pooh?

The bear hero of the popular book *Winnie-the-Pooh*. The story is about a toy bear who loves honey. It was written in 1926 by the English author A. A. Milne, who regularly visited a real American black bear named Winnie at the London Zoo.

The real-life Winnie first belonged to a Canadian Army captain, Harry Colebourn. He bought it as a cub in 1914 and named it Winnipeg (Winnie for short) after his home city. Captain Colebourn later gave the bear to the London Zoo.

London crowds—including A. A. Milne—loved Winnie. Tame and gentle, the bear even gave youngsters rides around the zoo. Thanks to Milne, Winnie now lives forever.

Grizzly bears

# INDEX

American black bear    6, 9, 11, 12, 13, 21, 23, 28, 29, 44
Arcturus    42
Asiatic black bear    5, 23, 32, 33
Asiatic brown bear    18
bamboo    30
bear attacks    14, 33, 39, 45
brown bears    8, 11, 13, 23, 25
camouflage    19
cave bears    22–23
claws    15, 29
communication    20–21
constellations    42–43
Coos Indians    40
cubs    8–11, 20
Cult of the Bear    40
day beds    13, 33, 37, 39
dens    6–7
dog bear, see sun bear
enemies    11, 22, 29
European brown bear    17
food    7, 10, 13, 25, 26
fossils    22
fur    19, 26, 35
giant panda    19, 23, 30–31

grizzly bear    10, 14, 21, 24–25, 47
guard hairs    19
hearing    13
hibernation    4
honey    13, 35
Hopi Indians    40
hunting    22, 29
Inuit    40
Kodiak bear    25
lesser pandas    30
life span    19
Malay bear, see sun bear
mating    20
molting    19
moon bear, see Asiatic black bear
National Parks    29
paws    16, 25, 26, 30
people and bears    3, 22, 30, 40–46
polar bears    7, 11, 13, 20, 23 26–27, 40
prey    15, 16
Pueblo Indians    40

red pandas    30
running    16
salmon    24, 25
sight    13
size    8, 11, 25, 39
sleep    4, 7–8
sloth bear    23, 34–35
smell    13
Smokey Bear    46
species    23
spectacled bear    23, 36–37
sun bear    23, 38–39
swimming    16, 26
teddy bear    46
teeth    13, 19, 30
territory    19, 21
trained bears    45
underfur    19
Ursa Major    42–43
Ursa Minor    42–43
Ute Indians    40
weight    8, 25, 29, 39
Winnie-the-Pooh    46
Yokuts Indians    40
zoos    19

## About the Authors

The Bergers agree with the Native American who said, "Bears are wiser than humans. They can live all winter without food or water!" "We hope that humans are wise enough," the authors say, "to protect bears and the wild places where these magnificent animals live."

## About the Illustrator

Roberto Osti has seen a bear up close. He says, "One day I was fishing in a small stream. A deer leaped across the stream. Soon a big black bear jumped into the water, stood on its hind legs sniffing the air, and then charged after the deer. I was in awe!"